WHAT OTHERS ARE SAYING:

"It's quick reading, easy to follow and can unleash a host of other questions that might never have crossed your mind—until it's too late. Consider it required reading in this school of hard knocks." **—Rocky Mountain News**

"The success or failure of a divorce is directly proportional to one's degree of survival. This book will increase the odds." **—Jan L. Warner, Fellow, American Academy of Matrimonial Lawyers; Member, National Academy of Elder Law Attorneys; President of Life Management and Solosource, Columbia SC.**

*"Boy, I wish I had seen this book earlier!"***—Divorced Mother**

*"This book fulfills the need for an easy-to-understand overview of the divorce process—an invaluable aid in entering the world of divorce."***—Barbara Stark, Attorney, Member of American Academy of Matrimonial Lawyers.**

"This book saved me hundreds of dollars in attorneys fees." **—Quote from letter**

*"This easy to read book provides basic answers to most of the questions frequently asked. I would recommend professional people keep copies of this book available for their clients to read and use."***—Dr. Bruce Fisher, Author of *Rebuilding*, Creator of Fisher Divorce Seminars, President of Family Relations Learning Center**

The SURVIVAL MANUAL *for* WOMEN *in* DIVORCE

The SURVIVAL MANUAL *for* WOMEN *in* DIVORCE

185 Questions and Answers About Your Rights and:
Common Property • Child Custody • Alimony & Debt
Child Support • Retirement Benefits • Much More!

CAROL ANN WILSON

Certified Financial Planner and Financial Divorce Specialist

& EDWIN SCHILLING III

Attorney at Law

First Printing 1990
Second Printing 1993
Third Printing 1994
Fourth Printing 1999
Fifth Printing 2004

ISBN 0-96267-906-2

Printed in the United States

Published by Omni Press
Boulder, CO 80301

Money's never mentioned
When speaking of romance
But say the word "divorce"
And you're talking high finance.

—*Charles Ghigna*

ABOUT THE AUTHORS

CAROL ANN WILSON, Certified Financial Planner® and Financial Divorce Specialist, is widely recognized as an expert in divorce planning. Wilson works as a pre-divorce financial consultant and expert witness in court. Ms. Wilson is the developer of a computer software program which is widely used by attorneys and financial planners to calculate financially equitable agreements. In 1993, she founded the Institute for Certified Divorce planners to train attorneys, CPAs and financial professionals in the financial issues of divorce. Currently, she is President of the Financial Divorce Association, Inc.

Wilson is the author of the *Financial Guide to Divorce Settlement* and coauthor of *The Survival Manual for Men in Divorce, Dollars and Sense of Divorce,* and *ABCs of Divorce for Women.* She has received national medial attention in magazines, newspapers, radio and television talk shows. For more information, visit www. carolannwilson.com.

 The law offices of EDWIN C. SCHILLING III (JD, CFP®) advises attorneys and individuals nationwide on the valuation and division of retirements incident to divorce. He has consulted on over 2500 cases in all 50 states and has testified in over 100 trials in 27 jurisdictions across the nation.

Schilling has testified before Congress on retirement division legislation and has presented over 100 programs on the complex issues of divorce law. He is the coauthor of *The Survival Manual for Men in Divorce* and *Dollars and Sense of Divorce,* and has published numerous articles for professional journals.

Schilling served as a judge advocate in the USAF and retired in the rank of colonel, and has specialized experience in military and other federal retirements. He is admitted to practice in Alaska, Colorado and Louisiana. He can be reached at P.O. Box 441485, Aurora, CO 80044, phone (303) 755-5121.

CONTENTS

PREFACE

A chat with Ed and Carol Ann.....

We wish that there were no need for this book.

>—We wish that attorneys did not have to spend their time negotiating over who will have the children at Christmas and who will get the family photo albums.

>—We wish that Financial Planners did not have to work out details for the sale of homes and divisions of hard earned retirement plans.

>—We wish that clergy, therapists, teachers, and guidance counselors did not have to spend their valuable time trying to put lives back together again.

>—We wish that tens of millions of Americans did not have to endure the pain of divorce.

But divorce is a reality—a reality repeated over one million times per year. Sometimes, despite the best efforts of good people, marriages break up.

Unfortunately, in our experience, ignorance is also a reality.

But ignorance does not have to be a reality.

Based upon the questions we are asked we saw that there was a need for a simple, straight-forward book on divorce. There are books on the market that go into great detail about the emotional, financial, and legal aspects of divorce. But many times all that is needed is a brief explanation, in plain English, of the basics of the divorce process.

We believe this is that book.

FOREWORD

WHO needs this book?

Anyone going through a divorce or separation.

WHAT can it do for me?

Give you a general understanding of the divorce process.

WHAT will it not do for me?

Give you all you need to know to represent yourself. By necessity, some answers are in general terms because the law varies from state to state. Always depend on your lawyer for advice.

WHEN do I need to read it?

As soon as you see there is a problem in your marriage.

HOW do I use it?

In one sitting, read all of the questions and answers. Then scan the Appendix to see what's in it. Then go back and concentrate on the areas that interest you. Finally, keep it handy as a reference.

WHY was this book written?

Because there was a need for a concise explanation of the divorce process in everyday language.

INTRODUCTION

Each year, 1.1 million people divorce in the United States. That's at least 2.2 million people who must face the challenges a break up can cause—not counting their children, in-laws, relatives, and friends.

Caught in the emotional turmoil of a divorce, many wives leave important questions unanswered. In fact, the last thing some women consider is their pocket book, even while they're beginning to sink in financial quicksand. Here are just a few examples we've come across in our practices.

—Claire divorced her full colonel husband after 26 years of marriage. The court didn't award her any of his military pension—worth over half a million dollars during his lifetime. What she did receive was maintenance of $250 per month for six years.

—Margaret's husband invested a lot of money during their marriage. When they divorced, he suggested that they simply split the investments fifty-fifty. Margaret agreed. But what she didn't know was that she was getting all the investments with a tax recapture. That meant she had to pay a whopping $18,000 tax bill.

—Shelly got the $220,000 family home while her husband received the other assets. But the house had a mortgage of $130,000 with payments of $1700 per month. That was more than Shelly was earning, so she put the house up for sale. Meanwhile, the real estate prices in her area were depressed, so she had to keep cutting her price. She finally sold the house for $145,000. Her asset which started at $90,000 had dwindled to $15,000—not counting selling costs.

—Gladys, a 53 year old homemaker had never worked outside the home. The judge in her divorce deemed her employable if she would take two years of training from the local vocational school, and he awarded her three years of "rehabilitative maintenance." Two years later, Gladys was looking for work. No job experience. Fifty-five years old. And the market just wasn't interested in her.

It doesn't have to be that way. With knowledge, planning and foresight, you can prepare for the financial impact of divorce—and win.

During the past decade, Ed Schilling and Carol Ann Wilson have worked with hundreds of people in the middle of divorce. We haven't seen it all—but we've seen a lot. We've used our experience and our expertise to give you an overview of the financial and legal issues you'll face—and give you the facts you need to come out on top.

Marriage creates economic inequality.

Consider these statistics:

In the first year after a divorce, the women's standard of living often drops by 33 percent, while the husband's increases.

Another fact: the higher the income of the family, the wider the gap between partners.

The reason? Most couples still invest in the husband's career while the wife's job takes second place. Even though society is changing, this pattern still holds for most couples. And if the marriage lasted a long time, the wife has lost at least a decade of career growth.

The courts often ignore this crucial issue when dividing marital property. Typically, divorce settlements divide only the tangible marital assets—the house, the car, the furniture. For most divorcing couples, this marital estate is not very large, averaging less than $20,000.

On the other hand, many courts traditionally overlook one major asset of a marriage—the husband's career and career assets. These include his:

> salary
> pension or retirement plan
> stock options
> health, life and disability insurance
> vacations
> sick pay
> education and training
> seniority and networking
> potential earning power.

Unfortunately, many courts don't recognize career assets as property. So, even when a wife has worked to put a husband through law school or sacrificed her interests—*invested* in her spouse's assets—she gets nothing in return.

At the same time, the courts expect equal independence from both partners. Sometimes the court will award rehabilitative maintenance to ease a spouse into the work force. But the courts base these settlements on the assumption—often false—that both spouses can be equally self-sufficient. Instead, women who have spent 20 or 30 years in traditional marriages find themselves out in the cold with no marketable skills and no real job prospects.

You can take action. With detailed financial planning, you can solve these and other problems. When you're trying to work out a fair settlement, remember that the court divides property only once, but career assets continue to produce income for years.

While you take that into account, your strategy should also include such factors as earnings, inflation, division of property, the amount and the length of maintenance, and reduced standards of living. If it's clear that one person will have surplus dollars from earnings, make sure this is considered when the court is making property settlements and maintenance arrangements.

Of course, we can't cover all the dimensions surrounding a divorce. But what this book can do is help answer questions—and bring up some important issues you may not have thought about. We hope you'll use this information to protect yourself, provide for your children and build for the future.

1

GETTING STARTED

If you're like most people, a divorce will be the first event that brings you in front of a judge. This section will tell you what you can expect during a divorce trial. We'll go over some of the alternatives to a trial, and outline other choices you have—options that may be easier, cheaper and still answer the challenges you're facing.

1. **What is a divorce?**

   A divorce is a civil action to terminate a marriage. It is also called Dissolution of Marriage.

2. **Do we both file for divorce?**

   Only one spouse need file. Or both can file as co-petitioners. The person who files is called the petitioner or the plaintiff. The spouse who is served is called the respondent or defendant.

3. **Where can I file for divorce?**

   Most states require that one of the parties be a legal resident of the state for a certain period of time before it will grant a divorce. This means that you may be able to choose where the case will be heard. Talk to an attorney about the possible choices you have.

4. Can we get divorced without an attorney?

Yes, but it is not recommended. If you have agreed on a final property settlement, have an attorney for each of you look it over and put it into legal language.

5. Can we both use the same attorney?

It is not recommended. If you do use your spouses' attorney, remember that this attorney represents your spouse, not you, if the going gets rough.

6. What are the grounds for filing for divorce?

Although the specific label varies from state to state, most states now permit a divorce if the marriage is "irretrievably broken." Other terms used are "irreconcilable differences" or "incompatibility." This is a "no fault" divorce. (See Appendix C.)

7. What does "no-fault" mean?

It means that it is not necessary, or permitted, to show that one party or the other did something wrong, or was "at fault", such as committing adultery.

8. What if my spouse won't give me a divorce?

The judge is the person who grants a divorce, not your spouse. Once you have filed for divorce, your attorney will serve a copy of the summons and complaint on your spouse. If no answer is filed within the time permitted by law in your state (for example 30 days) you will probably be granted a divorce by default. If your spouse contests the divorce action, a hearing will be set during which the two of you can testify and the judge can decide what the truth is.

9. What if my spouse is physically abusive?

Seek help immediately!!! You owe it to yourself and your children to resolve this before someone is seriously hurt.

10. Where should I go for help?

Call your local mental health facility or crisis line for assistance. They can make the necessary referrals. If you are afraid of serious bodily harm, you should call the police.

11. How long does it take to get divorced?

That varies from state to state. In some states, it takes 90 days after filing which is called the "cooling off period".

12. Then what?

If the divorce is friendly and a settlement is reached, the paperwork is filed and the divorce is complete. This is called the permanent order. If an agreement is not reached, a court date is set and a judge or other court official hears the case.

13. What if we want to settle out of court but we can't quite reach an agreement?

You can consider arbitration, negotiation or mediation.

14. What is arbitration?

Arbitration is the hiring of a private judge to hear your case. The advantage is getting a date more quickly as opposed to waiting for a court date.

15. What is negotiation?

In negotiation you may have four parties present: both spouses and each of their attorneys. A discussion is held until an agreement is reached.

16. What is mediation?

The two spouses meet with a neutral third party who is a trained mediator. The mediator does not give legal advice but gives legal information to help the two spouses reach an agreement. Mediation should be used when you believe the two of you can reason things out and you are not hostile toward each other. It can be viewed as an alternative between doing it yourself and going to court.

17. What if we agree on everything except how to divide up some of our property. Does the judge need to hear all the details of our case?

No. The judge only needs to hear the unresolved issues and make a ruling on that part. This can turn a 1 or 2 day trial into a 1 or 2 hour trial.

18. What are temporary orders?

Temporary orders tell what happens between the time the divorce is filed and the time that it is finished regarding child custody, child support, alimony, etc.

19. What are permanent orders?

Permanent orders are the final orders issued by the court which are binding on both parties and end the divorce negotiations. The divorce is now final.

20. What is court trial like for a divorce?

You will each be present with your attorneys. There will be opening arguments and closing arguments and direct examination and cross examination of witnesses called by each side. There may also be expert witnesses who have been ordered to appear.

21. What is direct examination?

It is when the attorney who called the witness asks the questions.

22. What is cross examination?

It is when the opposing attorney asks the questions.

23. What is an uncontested case?

An uncontested case is one in which the respondent does not oppose what the petitioner wants.

24. What is a deposition?

A deposition is the taking of testimony in preparation for the trial. Usually both attorneys, the witness and a court reporter are present.

25. What is discovery?

Discovery is the process of obtaining information, including documents, from the other side. For example, information about your spouse's checking account or retirement plan could be obtained through discovery.

26. What if I don't agree with the Judge's ruling?

In some instances, you may appeal. Your lawyer can explain whether or not it is available in your case and also what it may cost.

27. What should be included in my decree?

Your decree should include everything that you need to completely protect your rights. (See Appendix A.)

28. What is a Financial Divorce Specialist?

A Financial Divorce Specialist is a new type of professional. This person is often a Certified Financial Planner who has taken additional intensive training to become skilled in working with the financial issues in divorce including tax issues, retirement plans, division of property, and the financial effects of alimony and child support. They can appear as an expert witness if needed. For the name of a Financial Divorce Specialist in your area, call tollfree 888-332-3342 or visit the website: *www. FinancialDivorceAssociation.com.*

29. Can I resume the use of my maiden name at the time of the divorce?

Yes. You may ask for the right to resume your maiden name in the divorce papers your attorney files for you. This is routinely granted by the judge. Even if you do not ask for your maiden name back at the time of the divorce, you can file for resumption of your maiden name after the divorce is granted.

2

SEPARATION AGREEMENTS

You've probably heard the phrase "We're separated" a hundred times, but never—until now—wondered what it really meant. This chapter will tell you what a separation agreement can do for you and what it can't.

30. What is a separation agreement?

It is a contract between a husband and wife in which they agree to resolve such matters as property division, debts, custody and support when they separate from each other.

31. Who prepares a separation agreement?

It is best to have an attorney prepare one for you.

32. Can we divide our property in a separation agreement?

Yes. The two of you can agree upon a division of property in your separation agreement and that agreement will be binding. The property to be divided consists of real property (such as land and the buildings on it), tangible personal property (such as cars, jewelry and furniture) and intangible personal property (such as bank accounts, stocks and bonds, vested pensions and life insurance.)

33. Do I have to have a separation agreement?

The law does not require a couple to execute a separation agreement, but it is a wise idea if there are debts, children, support claims or property involved and the parties want to settle these matters in writing.

34. Does my spouse have to sign a separation agreement?

An "agreement" means that both parties sign voluntarily. You cannot compel your spouse to sign a separation agreement or to agree to the terms you wish to impose on him or her in the agreement.

35. Does a separation agreement help me to get a divorce?

Some states have provisions in their laws which might make divorce faster or easier if there is a separation agreement.

36. Can we settle in our separation agreement who would claim the tax exemption for our children?

Yes. The general rule is that the parent who has custody for more than half the year will claim the exemption, but the custodial parent may waive the exemption by signing the declaration on IRS Form 8332. The non-custodial parent attaches the declaration to his or her tax return and claims the exemption for the child.

37. Can I get my spouse for contempt of court if he/she breaks the promises in the separation agreement?

No. It is not contempt of court to violate a separation agreement unless the agreement has been made a part of a court order. Contempt of court is the failure to obey a court order without legal justification. You may, however, sue your spouse for breach of contract if he or she violates the separation agreement.

38. Will a separation agreement free me from paying debts for which I have signed along with my spouse?

No. A separation agreement is only a contract between spouses. It cannot bind third parties (such as banks or finance companies) that have not signed it. If, however, your spouse promises to pay a bill and then breaks that promise, resulting in your having to pay, you can then sue your spouse for breach of contract for the amount of money you had to pay.

39. Will a separation agreement stop my spouse from hassling me?

While separation agreements usually have a non-harassment clause in them, you should understand that no piece of paper—be it agreement or court order—is going to stop a person from doing something he or she wants to do. If the problem is one of physical violence, a court order would be more effective than a separation agreement and could be used to punish the wrongdoer if he or she violated the order.

40. Is a court of law bound by what we put in the separation agreement about our children?

No. The terms you include for child support, custody and visitation can always be altered or modified by the court in the best interests of the children. In the absence of proof to the contrary, however, there is a presumption that the terms concerning the children in your agreement are fair, reasonable and necessary for the best interests and welfare of the children.

41. Can the court modify the terms we include in a separation agreement concerning ourselves?

Unlike the terms concerning children, which are always modifiable by the court, the terms in a separation agreement that pertain to adults cannot be modified by the court except in very limited circumstances.

42. Can a single attorney do the separation agreement for me and my spouse?

It is always best to have two attorneys involved, one to advise each partner. In this way, the husband and the wife both know that they have received independent legal advice for their individual situation from a lawyer who does not have a conflict of interest in trying to represent two clients with different goals and needs.

3

PROPERTY

You may think you already know all about property. But do your views meet legal tests? What's yours, after all? Your joint savings account? The house that's in his name, even though you paid for half of it? And what about the all-important difference between traditional and career assets? We'll cover these questions, and you'll find out how to protect what belongs to you.

43. What is property?

Property includes assets such as: family home, rental property, cars, bank accounts, mutual funds, stocks and bonds, IRAs, retirement plans, collections, etc.

44. What kinds of property are there?

Although the details vary from state to state, property is usually divided into separate and marital.

45. What is separate property?

There are three kinds of separate property. Separate property is:
1. What you bring into the marriage
2. What you inherit during the marriage
3. What you receive during the marriage as a gift

46. What is marital property?

Marital property is any property acquired during the marriage, no matter whose name it's in, and in many states, the increase in value of the separate property.

47. What is an example of separate property that is the kind that you bring into a marriage?

Example 1:
Assume that you owned a house before you were married and it was titled in your name only. This house had a fair market value of $100,000 and the mortgage was $80,000. This asset, as long as the title stays in your name, will always be considered separate property.

Example 2:
Assume that when you were married, you had a savings account with $1000 titled in your name only. This savings account, as long as it is in your name only, is separate property.

48. What is an example of separate property that you inherit during your marriage?

Assume your father died and left you $10,000. If this money is put into an account in your name only, that can be kept as separate property.

49. What is an example of separate property that I receive during the marriage as a gift?

Assume that your mother gave you a gift of $10,000 and the check was made out to you only and not to you and your spouse. You put it into a savings account with your name only on the account. This gift would be considered separate property.

50. If my husband put $1500 in a savings account in his name only during our marriage, is that considered marital property?

It depends on where the money came from. As we have seen above, it may be his separate property. But if it is money that he earned, it would be marital property even though he put it in an account that is only in his name.

51. Regarding the $1000 in my savings account that I brought into the marriage as separate property, it is now worth $1100 and we are getting a divorce. How much of this is separate property and how much is marital property?

The original $1000 that was brought in as personal property is still considered separate property. The $100 interest that has been added to that savings account is the increase in value and in many states is considered marital property.

52. What if the $1000 that I bring into the marriage as personal property is added to some money with my spouse and we buy a house?

The $1000 is now part of a marital asset and the house is considered to be a marital asset.

53. What if I bring a house into the marriage that is in my name only, but I add my spouses name to the Deed?

Then the whole house is considered marital property. You have made a "presumptive gift" to the marriage.

54. What if I take my $1000 savings account and buy a CD with my name only on it. Then I sell the CD and put it back into a savings account in my name only. Is this still separate property?

Yes. As long as you can trace those funds and they have always been kept separate and in your name only, then this is considered separate property.

55. What if I had taken the $1000 from my savings account and my spouse and I bought a rental house together and I added that $1000 to the down payment of the rental house. Then we sold the rental house. I got my $1000 back and put it into a savings account in my name only. Is that still my separate property?

It depends on your state. Some states would say that under these facts, the $1000 has retained its separate identity. Other states would say that these funds have changed in nature. You have comingled or mixed them with marital property. At that time, they can never go back to be personal property.

56. My husband gave me a 4-karat engagement ring which, by definition, would make it personal property because it was a gift. My husband says that that size diamond was something he considered to be an investment and so it's marital property. Who is right?

I'm sorry, but that's one for the judge to decide.

57. What if I inherit $10,000 and buy a car for the whole family to enjoy and it is titled in my name only. Is that still separate property?

It depends on how the judge will look at what you did. He may conclude you made a gift of this to the family and consider it marital property.

58. How will the judge divide our property?

There is a presumption in most states that the fairest split would be an even division of all the marital property, regardless of who has title to the property, who paid for it, and so on. Under certain circumstances, however, the judge might decide that a 50/50 split is not fair to one or both of the parties. A number of factors may be considered. For example, he many consider such matters as monetary and homemaker contributions to the marriage by each party, tax consequences of an unequal division, whether alimony or child support is presently being paid and so on. (See Appendix G.)

59. In a 50/50 property split, do we divide each asset in half?

Not necessarily. You can trade assets against each other. If this is not possible, you can set up a property settlement note.

60. What is a property settlement note?

A property settlement note is used when there are insufficient assets or cash for one party to buy out the other party's interest in an asset. In essence, using a promissory note, the party who wants an asset borrows the money from the party who owns the asset.

You decide on the number of years, the interest rate and the monthly amount to be paid. It is not taxable to the recipient like alimony as it is still considered a division of property. The interest, however, does have to be declared as taxable income.

Property settlement notes should be collateralized as they do not survive bankruptcy.

61. Can you give me an example?

Yes. Suppose the wife wants to keep the house. The value of the husband's interest is $15,000 and there are no other assets for the wife to give to the husband in exchange for his interest. Instead of going to a bank to borrow the money, the wife would sign a promissory note for $15,000 with the husband as the creditor.

62. I have heard the terms "traditional" and "career" assets. What are these?

Traditional assets are things like the house, cars, furniture, savings accounts, checking accounts, stocks, bonds, investments, real estate and rental property, limited partnerships, etc.

63. What are career assets?

Career assets include the education or training, the license or degree, job experience, seniority, life insurance, health insurance, disability insurance, unemployment, social security, paid sick leave, vacation, pension plans, retirement plans, network of professional contacts, etc.

64. Is there value to a college degree or education in a marriage?

Some states do give value to the degree as a marital asset. Other states don't. You need to check the law in your own state.

65. What about a doctor's degree or an attorney's profession?

Again, depending on the state, the profession may or may not be a marital asset. Certainly, the increased earning power from this profession is given weight in the final decisions.

66. How do you value household goods?

The value is Fair Market Value; in other words, what someone will pay for it at a garage sale.

67. Should the wife get the house?

Not necessarily. It depends on the personal and financial factors involved.

Example 1: If the wife has custody of the children, it may be best for her to keep the house for at least a few more years to keep changes to a minimum for the children.

Example 2: If the house payment is high and the wife does not have a high income, she may need to move to a place with a lower monthly payment.

Example 3: If the house payment is very low, it may be best for the wife to stay in the house.

Example 4: If the equity in the house represents her portion of the assets and the husband gets all the liquid assets, she may find herself later with no cash and unable to buy groceries with the equity in the house.

68. What if we can't agree on the value of our house?

A real estate appraiser needs to be called in and an appraisal needs to be done.

69. Do we subtract a selling commission from the value?

Many judges will not allow the selling commission to be subtracted. However, if the house is already up for sale, it probably can be deducted.

70. What does "basis in the house" mean because I've heard it can affect my settlement.

Basis is generally the cost of the house and is not related to the remaining balance of the mortgage. The basis may be affected by improvements, sales costs and sales of previous homes. Therefore you may want to have a CPA verify the basis before you agree on your settlement.

71. How can the basis affect my settlement?

If the house is sold, the basis and the sales price will determine the taxable gain (capital gain) and the amount of income tax owed on the gain.

72. Tell me more about capital gain.

When you and your spouse sell your jointly owned residence, you will be able to take a $500,000 exclusion from any capital gain. Capital gain is the profit resulting from the sale of capital investments, such as stocks and real estate. It has nothing to do with the mortgage on the property. A single person can take a $250,000 exclusion.

73. This all sounds so complicated. Do I really need to pay attention to this?

Absolutely. If you are planning to sell your house at the time of divorce, you need to have a CPA analyze the tax consequences of any proposed sale or transfer of ownership between the parties.

For example:
If you get the house with a basis of $35,000 and sell it for $420,000, your taxable gain could be $385,000. After your $250,000 exclusion, your taxable gain is $135,000. Without proper planning, you could end up owing $20,250 in federal taxes.

74. Is there a tax break for older people when they sell a house?

Not any more. You may be remembering the one-time exclusion at age 55 of $125,000. But with the tax reform act of 1996, that is no longer available.

75. Can we subtract capital gains taxes from the value of the house?

Most judges will not allow this as they feel it is speculative. However, if the house is to be sold immediately, the capital gain taxes should be considered.

76. Is life insurance an asset?

If there is cash value, yes. Do not confuse the death benefit with cash value. Cash value is found in "permanent" policies such as whole life or universal life. Term life insurance does not have cash value.

77. Is term life insurance on an uninsurable person ever considered an asset?

Some attorneys will argue that a large insurance policy on someone who can no longer buy insurance should be considered in final negotiations.

78. What if my spouse is spending the assets?

Tell your attorney as soon as possible.

79. What if my spouse is hiding assets?

Let your attorney know what you think they are, and a special legal action can be brought to try to discover those assets.

80. What if there is a family business?

This will probably need to be appraised by an experienced appraiser or a CPA.

81. What if I suspect that my spouse who runs the family business is hiding information from me?

Start making copies of as much financial information as you can get your hands on. This includes:

- Bank statements
- Canceled checks and checkbooks
- Savings account passbooks
- Income tax returns (both personal and business)
- Estate and gift tax returns
- Financial reports
- Applications for loans
- Income and Balance Sheets for the business

4

PENSION AND RETIREMENT PLANS

Often, a pension plan is the most valuable property a couple has. But many people don't even know how much their spouse's retirement is worth. Here, you'll read about the two types of retirement plans, and learn about some of the ways courts divide them.

82. Are pension plans and retirement plans marital assets?

Yes.

83. How do I find out how much the pension plan is worth?

There are several ways:

1. The company itself send out a written report in the first quarter of each calendar year.
2. The company can be asked for the present value of the pension plan.
3. A CPA or Financial Divorce Specialist can be asked to do a pension evaluation.

84. What does vesting mean?

Vesting means that at least some of the pension belongs to the individual and not the company. Practically speaking it is what the person would get if he/she left the company. This share of the pension comes from two sources:

1. Employee contributions are 100% vested immediately. When an employee leaves a company whether by his choice or not, he can take 100% of his contributions plus any earnings on those contributions.
2. Employer contributions can be anywhere between 0% - 100% vested. Assume the employer has contributed $3,000 to the employee's account and it has earned $500 in interest. Assume the employee is 10% vested and then decides to leave the company or is fired. The employee can take 10% of the $3,500 total value of the account or $350.

85. What if my husband's pension plan says he will receive $1,200 per month when he retires at age 65 but doesn't give a current value of the pension plan?

This is a Defined Benefit plan.

86. What is a Defined Benefit plan?

A Defined Benefit plan is an account that the employer contributes to in various amounts to guarantee that the employee receives a certain amount at retirement time.

87. How do I find out what this Defined Benefit plan is worth now as a marital asset?

In one of 2 ways:
1. The company can be asked for the present value of the pension plan.
2. A CPA or Financial Divorce Specialist can be asked to do a pension evaluation.

88. What if he dies soon after retirement?

Survivor benefits can be set up before retirement—even for an ex-spouse. If survivor benefits are chosen, the monthly payout is usually a smaller amount since the account will now pay out for two lives.

89. What if my ex-husband dies before he is eligible to receive the monthly benefit?

Each pension needs to be evaluated as to its rules. In some cases, the pension may disappear and no one will get anything.

90. What is a QDRO?

QDRO stands for Qualified Domestic Relations Order. It is used to divide a pension in a divorce. A spouse can be awarded anywhere from 0% to 100% of a pension in a QDRO. The most common amount is 50%.

91. How do I get my portion of the retirement plan?

It depends on the type of plan:

Example 1: If the retirement plan has cash now, it can be divided into 2 parts—one part for the employee and one part for the spouse. The spouse's part can be taken in cash. Example: John is 52 years old. His 401K plan has $320,000 cash in it. A 50% portion according to a QDRO ($160,000) will be awarded to Mary, age 50. The other $160,000 will remain in John's account.

Example 2: If the retirement plan is a Defined Benefit plan and has no cash value now, at the time of retirement of the employee, the spouse will receive a percent of the payout. Example: Bill, age 56, is to receive $1,200 per month upon retirement at age 65. If there is a 50% split according to a QDRO, Bill will receive $600 per month at retirement and his ex-wife, Sara, will receive $600 per month at that time. If Bill, between the ages of

31

56 and 65 earns a higher retirement payout, Sara will still receive $600 per month which is her half of the marital portion (the value at the time of divorce) and Bill will receive the remainder.

92. If Mary in Example #1 takes the $160,000 cash, will she have to pay the 10% penalty because she spent it before age 59 1/2?

A divorce court order giving Mary a portion of a qualified retirement plan is the only time that Mary can spend qualified pension funds and not have to pay the penalties that might have been due because she is not yet 59 1/2 years old. Be sure to seek the advice of a CPA or a Financial Divorce Specialist.

93. Will Mary have to pay income taxes on this $160,000?

Without proper financial planning, the $160,000 will be considered ordinary income and will be taxed accordingly.

94. Can Mary do anything to avoid paying taxes now?

Mary could rollover the funds into an IRA, which will then follow regular IRA rules.

5

MAINTENANCE AND ALIMONY

Alimony. You've all heard the word. But what does it really mean? Do you have to pay taxes on it? What are "reasonable needs" and how will that important qualifier affect you? For the ammunition you need to assure yourself of the best settlement, read on.

95. What is the difference between maintenance and alimony?

Practically speaking, there is no difference. This is just a difference in terminology. With the "no fault" divorce laws, the word maintenance is more commonly used. (See Appendix C.)

96. Who pays the taxes on maintenance?

Normally, the person who receives maintenance pays taxes on it as ordinary income. The person who pays maintenance gets to deduct that amount from their taxable income.

97. How do I know if I qualify to receive maintenance?

You qualify for maintenance if you are unable to meet your reasonable needs.

98. What does "reasonable needs" mean?

Look at the property division. If Sara and John have been married 40 years and Sara is 60 years old and has never worked, she seems to be a candidate for maintenance. If, on the other hand, she receives a two million dollar property settlement, there may not be a reasonable need.

99. Can the husband ever receive maintenance?

Yes, if he shows reasonable need and the wife is able to pay.

100. Are there different types of maintenance?

There are 2 types: open-ended and non-modifiable.

101. What is open-ended maintenance?

Open-ended maintenance is open to review. It can be increased, decreased or stopped as circumstances change.

102. What is non-modifiable maintenance?

Non-modifiable maintenance is paid for exactly as long as is stated — no less, no more.

103. What if I am awarded maintenance for 6 years, but my spouse dies in 2 years?

Maintenance will stop upon death of the payor.

104. How do I protect my maintenance in the event of the death of my ex-spouse?

The court order should contain provisions for life insurance to cover the life of the person paying the maintenance.

105. **What if I am awarded maintenance for 6 years and I get remarried in 2 years?**

Open-ended maintenance usually terminates upon remarriage. Non-modifiable maintenance will be paid for 6 years even if there is remarriage. Check with your attorney to be sure.

106. **Does my husband have to pay maintenance if I am living with another man?**

Your husband must pay maintenance as long as a court order requires him to do so. Some orders provide that maintenance will stop under these circumstances. Check with your attorney if your husband has stopped making payments.

107. **What is permanent maintenance?**

So called "permanent maintenance" continues for life unless modified by the court.

108. **Are pre-nuptial agreements an important consideration?**

Yes, they could nullify all the rules we've been talking about.

6

CHILD SUPPORT

For parents, child support can be the key issue in a divorce, marking the line between making it or going under. We'll explain how it is figured, how long it can last and when it can be cut off.

109. Who pays the taxes on child support?

Child support is not taxable to the one who receives it, nor is it tax deductible by the one who pays it.

110. How do we figure how much child support should be paid?

Most states now have Child Support Guidelines. These should be consulted by you and your attorney in your own state. These guidelines take into account the gross earnings of each party, the expenses they are paying for the children, how much time each child spends with the parent, etc.

111. How long is child support paid?

Child support, without an agreement or court order, usually ends at the child's 18th or 19th birthday, although a separation agreement or court order by consent may set a lower or higher age, such as upon graduation from college or at age 21. If the child is disabled or handicapped, payment may be for life. Your attorney should explain this to you.

112. When my child is visiting the other parent, can he or she reduce child support paid to me?

Unless the court order or separation agreement specifically provides for a reduction, the child support payment should remain the same. Again, check with your attorney.

113. If I cannot see my child for visitation, can I stop paying child support?

In some states, denial of visitation is not legal justification for withholding child support. Neither is lack of child support a legal excuse for refusing the other parent visitation rights.

114. Can the other parent's paycheck be garnished for child support?

States vary in garnishment requirements and procedures and some states do not allow garnishment at all. Garnishment is a court proceeding that requires an attorney.

115. What if I need more child support in the future?

If the child support is set out in a court order, you may petition the court to increase child support if you can show that there has been a substantial change of circumstances.

116. What is a substantial change of circumstances?

Such a change usually consists of increased living expenses, inflation or an increase in the earnings of the other parent.

117. Can the child support increase each year to offset inflation?

Yes, if it is agreed to by the parents or written into the court order.

118. Can child support also be reduced?

Yes, if there has been a substantial change of circumstances. For example, a parent who just lost his job or has had a substantial reduction in pay could petition the court to reduce child support payments that he or she is making.

7

CHILD CUSTODY

Next to the actual decision to file for a divorce, custody may be the most emotionally-charged issue you'll face. We'll discuss some steps you can take to increase your chances of being granted custody, and address the issue of visitation rights.

119. Do mothers automatically get custody of their children when a separation occurs?

The courts of most states do not establish an automatic preference for either mother or father, but they do look very closely at which parent will best promote the welfare and interests of the children of the couple.

120. What kinds of factors do the courts consider in granting custody?

They usually look at who has primarily taken care of the child during the marriage (washing, feeding and clothing the child, for example, or helping the child with homework), who has the best approach to discipline, who has cared for the child since separation (if the couple has already separated), what work schedules either or both parents have, and how each parent can provide for the physical, emotional, educational, religious and social needs of the child.

121. Can a custody order be changed?

No custody order is ever "permanent." However, once a parent is awarded custody in a court order, the judge can change the custody order only if there is a substantial change in circumstances. Usually it must be proven that the change has a direct and adverse effect on the child.

122. Will my separation agreement protect me from the other parent snatching my child?

No. A separation agreement is only a contract between you and the other parent, not a court order. A court order is enforceable by contempt of court. Court orders of one state can be filed and registered in another state and thus be treated as if they were issued by the second state for purposes of enforcement . None of this applies to separation agreements.

123. If my spouse is granted custody, will I get visitation rights?

Ordinarily the noncustodial parent is entitled to reasonable visitation rights with a minor child except in extraordinary situations, such as when the noncustodial parent has a history of abusing the child. Visitation can be flexible and unstructured, assuming the parties can get along and agree on the times and terms of visitation, or it can be highly structured and rigid, with certain days and times set out with great specificity.

124. If the other parent does not like the present custody order, can he or she file for custody in another state?

Under the Uniform Child Custody Jurisdiction Act, which has been passed and made law in almost every state, the court in a custody case must always inquire into whether the child or children has been the subject of custody litigation in any other state.

When a judge finds that another court has made an award of custody, the judge should refuse to rule on the case and refer the parent to the court that originally entered the custody order.

125.   Won't custody be settled when I obtain a divorce?

Divorce decrees do not necessarily settle custody matters.

8

DEBT AND CREDIT CARDS

Perhaps you've heard the horror stories. A man runs up thousands of dollars of debt on a credit card after filing for divorce—and his wife pays. Another spouse tries to avoid paying child support by declaring bankruptcy. Here, you'll find out what you can do about these and other marital debts.

126. Are debts incurred while we were married the responsibility of both of us?

Generally Yes.

127. What about debts that my spouse incurs after I file for divorce?

Generally you are responsible for debts he incurs until the divorce is final.

128. What if my spouse is incurring astronomical debt?

A second hearing can be held to release you from that debt. But if that debt is not paid, the creditors may hold you legally liable.

129. Should I establish my own credit?

Yes. If possible, this should be done while the marriage is sound.

130. If my spouse files bankruptcy after divorce, will he still have to pay me child support and maintenance?

Yes. Although bankruptcy can complicate matters, the law says that child support and maintenance are not dischargeable debts in bankruptcy.

9

INSURANCE

Although insurance is designed to provide security, it can be one of the biggest causes of insecurity when a couple divorces. After reading this chapter you may decide to buy life insurance for your husband—even after you've divorced him.

131.   Will my husband's health insurance continue to cover the children and myself?

Most policies provide that the insurance will continue to cover the children until they are 21 years old but it will not cover you as an ex-wife.

132.   What is the COBRA law I have heard about?

COBRA (Consolidated Omnibus Budget Reconciliation Act of 1986) says that if your husband's company has at least 20 employees, they must allow you to apply to their health insurance company for continued coverage in your name for another 3 years.

133.   Will my husband pay this premium?

Only if he is ordered to do so by the court. Normally, you will need to pay this premium and if you ever miss a payment, they can drop you and will not reinstate you. So, make sure you make your premium payments.

134.   What if I am uninsurable and cannot get other health insurance?

Check with your existing insurance company to see if you can convert the existing insurance to your name only. Also, most states now have "uninsurable" insurance.

135.   My husband is going to get different car insurance on the vehicle he is taking. With expenses so high during this divorce, can I go ahead and cancel the existing insurance on his vehicle?

DON'T EVER CANCEL ANY INSURANCE WHILE THERE MAY STILL BE A NEED. Make sure the new insurance is in place before canceling any policy, even when you may have to double up on a monthly payment. The risk is just not worth it.

136.   The court told me to keep my ex-wife as beneficiary on my life insurance until our children are 21 years old, but I am marrying again and have a new family to support.

Unless you obtain a new court order, you will need to acquire an additional life insurance policy with your new family as the beneficiaries.

137.   What's the best way to find out about my coverage after divorce?

Read the policy and/or have the agent explain it to you.

138. When should I obtain life insurance on the life of my spouse?

Consider it when you will depend on payments from your former spouse for your own support or that of your children.

139. Is there any pitfall to watch out for in this area?

Yes. Before the divorce is final, make sure your spouse can pass an insurance physical and will cooperate in obtaining the policy.

10

SOCIAL SECURITY

B ecause so many people depend on Social Security payments to supplement their retirement, it makes sense to address this issue in your settlement. We'll talk about this often overlooked aspect of divorce, and you may discover that you're entitled to your spouse's Social Security—even if you didn't work outside the home.

140. If I have never worked, will I get Social Security?

If your spouse has worked and if you have been married for 10 years or more, then you are entitled to one-half of your spouse's Social Security or your own, whichever is higher.

141. If I worked for 5 years and have a very small amount in my Social Security account, how much Social Security will I receive at retirement?

If you were married for 10 years or more, you are entitled to half of your spouse's Social Security or yours, whichever is higher. You may make this choice at the time that you apply for your Social Security.

142. As the wife who has been married for 10 years, if my husband gets remarried, will I still be eligible for half of his Social Security?

If your husband gets remarried after you have been married for 10 years, you will still be entitled to half of his Social Security.

143. Will that reduce his Social Security?

No. It will not. Assume that he is entitled at age 65 to receive $750/mo in Social Security. He will still be able to get his $750/mo. You will be able to receive $375/mo.

144. As the wife who has been married for more than 10 years, and I get remarried, will I be able to receive half of my first husband's Social Security?

You now have a new husband and you are no longer entitled to your first husband's benefits.

The exception to this is that if you are married to your second husband 10 years or longer and then get divorced, you will be able to receive half of his Social Security upon retirement or half of your first husband's or your own account, whichever is higher. You have that choice at the time of retirement.

145. As a nonworking wife who has been married for 10 years or more, what happens if, after the divorce, my husband dies before he turns 65?

If you have not remarried by age 60, you will get his full Social Security benefits.

11

LAWYERS

Maybe you've already asked friends to recommend a lawyer. Or you've paged through a phone directory, wondering if there was a better way to find the right attorney for your case. Here, you'll discover the dos and donts of choosing a lawyer. We'll also offer some money-saving tips on how to get the most out of the time you spend with an attorney.

146.   How do I find an attorney?

It will take some work on your part, especially if you want to find an experienced domestic relations lawyer. But it will pay to shop around.

147.   Where do I start? Any suggestions?

1. Ask friends who have gone through a divorce if they have a recommendation.
2. Ask a member of the clergy.
3. Visit the courthouse and observe the lawyers in action. (A phone call to the clerk's office can get you the date and location of cases and hearings.)
4. Contact the American Academy of Matrimonial Lawyers,

Twenty North Michigan Avenue, Chicago, Illinois 60602, (312) 263-6477.

5. Contact the American Bar Association, 750 North Lakeshore Drive, Chicago, Illinois 60611, (312) 988-5000.

6. Go to a library and look through a volume called "Martindale Hubble." This monstrous book has listings of lawyers by city throughout the United States. Read the descriptions of the work the lawyer or firm does, and read the biographies. Look for statements that indicate the lawyer is "Board Certified in Domestic Relations or Family Law", and see if he/she is active in organizations for domestic relations lawyers. Although the listings and information are supplied and paid for by the lawyer, this book is an excellent method of narrowing down your choice.

7. Call the state bar association and ask if they have a listing of lawyers who are members of the "Family Law Section" who live in your area. Note: some states now have certified specialists in family law. Ask if your state has such a system and obtain the names of several in your area.

8. Call the local bar association, listed in the white pages of the phone book, and ask if they have a lawyer referral service for domestic relations lawyers. (Sometimes the number for the referral service will be in the yellow pages before or after the listings of lawyers.) Remember that a referral is not a recommendation as to the competence of the lawyer.

9. Use the yellow pages of the phone book. Read the ads, looking for an indication that the lawyer specializes or emphasizes divorce work.

148. What are some things that I should not do?

1. Don't use an attorney that is a family friend or business associate of your spouse. Divided loyalties will probably be a problem.

2. Don't use your spouses' lawyer. (If you do, remember that this lawyer represents your spouse, not you, if the going gets rough.)

3. Don't use a lawyer just because he/she has quoted you the lowest price.

149. Is it OK to shop around"?

Sure. You need to feel comfortable with the attorney that is going to represent you and you can only find this out by meeting the lawyer face to face. Remember, the decisions the lawyer makes will affect you the rest of your life.

150. How much will a divorce cost me?

It depends on how complicated the situation is, and how much disagreement there is between the parties.

151. Should I ask the lawyer how much he/she will charge?

Absolutely. This may be one of the first things you bring up. Don't be hesitant. The attorney should even bring this up if you don't. As stated, the cost will vary depending on the circumstances, so an exact figure may not be possible, but the lawyer should be able to give you a reasonably good estimate and explain how fees are calculated.

152. I've heard that many attorneys want a part or all of their fee in advance. Why is this?

It's "insurance" that the fee will be paid. In the domestic relations field, it is frequent that a person filing for divorce will change his/her mind and not pay for the work that has been done.

153. **What can I do to prepare for my first meeting with the lawyer?**

Good question. Since many charge on an hourly basis, the more time you spend in preparation, the less of his/her time you will take. Here are some items of information to write down:
  1. Information on your family such as name and ages of you, your spouse, and your children, when and where you were married, and how long you have lived in the county and state.
  2. Ballpark figures on your family's finances, such as income, expense, property, and life insurance.
  3. A summary of your marital problems
  4. See Appendix B for a complete list.

154. **What if I can't get some of this information from my spouse?**

Your attorney can subpoena this information which means getting it through legal channels. This can be expensive so it is helpful if each of you provide this information for each other.

155. **What questions should I ask my attorney?**

You should ask questions such as:
  1. How will I be charged?
  2. What are the types of expenses I will be liable for, and how much do you think these will run?
  3. How many divorce cases did you handle last year?
  4. What portion of your law practice is devoted to divorces?
  5. If we have to go to trial, what is your divorce trial experience?
  6. Will you handle the case yourself, or will an assistant do the work?
  7. What is expected of me?
  8. What can I do to help you?
  9. Tell me about temporary alimony and/or child support.

156. Who pays for my lawyer?

As a general rule, you must retain and pay for your own attorney in a divorce case.

157. What if I can't afford to hire a good attorney or expert witnesses because my husband handles the money?

It is typical that many women do not hire the help they need because for whatever reason, they feel they cannot pay for it. This divorce will affect your entire financial future and you cannot afford to scrimp now.

158. Any final hints?

Yes. First, tell your lawyer that you want him/her to tell you the good news and bad news, and not just what he/she thinks you want to hear. Secondly, don't use a lawyer unless you are comfortable with him/her. Depend on your "gut reaction", and if you don't feel comfortable, try someone else. Finally, don't use your lawyer as a therapist. They are not trained for such a role and will have to charge you for their time, even if you just want someone to listen to you.

12

TAX ISSUES

We cannot overstate the importance of relying on the advice of a professional who knows your individual situation. Not only do the laws change, but so do the interpretation of these laws.

159. How does marital status affect how I may file my tax return?

It is critical. If you are considered "married", you may file as "married filing a joint return" or "married filing a separate return", or "head of household". If you are considered "unmarried", your status will be "single" or possibly "head of household".

160. How do I determine if I am "considered unmarried"?

Your marital status is determined on the last day of the tax year, or December 31, for most individuals. In general, you are considered "unmarried" for the whole year if either of the following applies: (1) you have obtained a final decree of divorce or separate maintenance by the last day of the tax year; or (2) you obtained a degree of annulment which holds that no valid marriage ever existed.

161. Is there an exception?

How did you guess? Yes, although you are generally considered "married" if you are not divorced or legally separated, if you live apart from your spouse, under certain circumstances, you may be considered "unmarried" and can file as "head of household".

162. When may a married person living apart from a spouse file as "head of household"?

Generally when the following conditions are met: (1) the taxpayer maintains a household for his/her dependent child; (2) the household is the taxpayer's home and the main home of the dependent child for more than half the year; (3) the taxpayer provides more than 50% of the cost of maintaining the household; (4) the taxpayer's spouse was not a member of the household during the last six months of the year; and (5) the taxpayer is entitled to claim the child as a dependent.

163. Is it possible for each spouse to file as "head of household"?

Yes, if there are at least two children.

164. When would it be to my advantage to file as "head of household"?

This is a matter to discuss with a tax professional.

165. I've heard that I can be held liable for all the taxes if I sign a joint return even though my spouse actually prepared the return and earned all the income. Is this true?

It can be. Generally, both people who sign a joint return are jointly and individually liable for any tax, interest, or penalty that may be due. For example, one spouse may be held liable for all the tax due even if all the income was earned by the other spouse. The liability can even extend after you are divorced as to returns that were filed before the divorce. Exceptions are made in what is referred to as the "innocent spouse rule". Again, see your tax professional.

166. What if we file separate returns while we are married?

Each spouse is responsible for only the tax due on their own return. But note that in many cases the total tax liability for the couple will be higher if separate returns are filed.

167. In Question #96 you said that maintenance is taxed to the person who receives it and is deductible by the one who pays it, and in Question #109 you said that child support is not taxed to the one who receives it nor deductible by the one who pays it. Is it really that simple?

Not really. This is a very complex area of tax law. For example, for documents executed after 1984, a payment to or for a spouse under a divorce or separation document, is maintenance only if all the following requirements are met:
1. the spouses do not file a joint return,
2. payments are in cash, including checks or money orders,
3. the document does not say that the payments are not maintenance,
4. if the spouses are separated under a decree of divorce or separation, they are not members of the same household when the payment is made,
5. there is no liability to make any payment in cash or property after the death of the recipient spouse,
6. the payment is not treated as child support,
7. for documents executed in 1985 or 1986 "the minimum term rule is met".

168. Condition 6 in the previous question talks about confusing maintenance and child support. Isn't it really easy to tell the difference?

Not necessarily. An instrument can be drafted in such a manner that it is not clear what the payment is for. Surprisingly, this is a tricky area. For example, if something is called maintenance, but the order says that it is to be reduced when the child graduates from high school, the IRS may take the position that it was really child support for all the years in which it had been paid. And this would change the tax treatment of the payments.

169. If I am to live in the house after the divorce and my ex-husband is to continue making the mortgage payments, will they be considered maintenance? (I am assuming that all of the requirements in Question 167 have been met.)

It depends on how the title to the residence is held after the divorce.

170. What if he has title alone?

The mortgage payments are not considered to be maintenance. However, the ex-husband would be entitled to deduct the interest and real estate taxes if he itemized his deductions.

171. What if I have title alone after the divorce?

The payments by the ex-husband are considered to be maintenance.

172. I think our title says "tenants in common"—what are the rules for this case?

One-half of the mortgage payment would be treated as maintenance and the other half would not, but the ex-husband could deduct half of the real estate interest and taxes as an itemized deduction.

173.   What about payments for utilities?

If the ex-husband agrees to pay the utilities, these may qualify for alimony regardless of who owns the house.

174.   Who may deduct the medical expenses for a child as an itemized deduction?

Either parent who incurs the expense may deduct the expenses regardless of which parent is entitled to claim the child as a dependent or who has the custody of the child.

175.   What about the child care credit?

This can be tricky. Where the parents are divorced, legally separated or separated and live apart during the last six months of the year, the parent who has custody for the longer period of the year is entitled to the child care credit, regardless of which parent is entitled to claim the child as a dependent.

176.   Why did you say this can be tricky?

If the rule is misunderstood, the credit may be lost, even though the child care is actually paid for. Take the example of the case in which the child lives with the mother, but the father pays the child care provider directly, neither can claim the credit and it will be lost.

177.   Can I deduct any of the costs of getting a divorce?

Yes. Although you may not deduct legal fees and court costs for getting a divorce, you may be able to deduct legal fees paid for tax advice in connection with divorce.

178. Anything else?

Yes, you may be able to deduct fees you paid to appraisers, actuaries, financial planners and accountants for services in determining your correct tax or in helping to get maintenance.

179. How do I know what the fee I paid was used for?

For tax purposes, you should ask for a breakdown showing what service was performed and the fee paid.

180. This all seems very complicated. Are there any books I can read that will help me understand this better?

Yes. There are many good commercial tax guides that are available for around $10. In addition, there are a number of free tax publications available from the IRS. Your local IRS office can tell you how to obtain the forms. Here are a few:

Publication #	Name
17	Your Federal Income Tax
504	Tax Information for Divorced or Separated Individuals
521	Moving Expenses
523	Tax Information on Selling Your Home
590	Individual Retirement Arrangements

Note: We strongly suggest that you at least get Publications 17 and 504.

13

INDIVIDUAL RETIREMENT ACCOUNTS

181. Are our IRAs considered to be marital property?

Yes. They can be divided and transferred just like other pieces of property.

182. How can his IRA be transferred to me? Will there be penalties or taxes on the transfer?

The transfer is permitted because it is a result of a divorce court order. There are no penalties or taxes as long as the asset is put into your IRA within 60 days.

183. You said in Question 92 that she could take a portion of his pension plan, pay taxes but pay no penalty. Can she do the same with his IRA?

No. An IRA is not divisible by a QDRO (Qualified Domestic Relations Order) and therefore is not subject to the same rules. If she is under the age of 59 1/2, she will have to pay the 10% penalty in addition to the taxes on the amount taken out if she doesn't put the money into her own IRA within 60 days or if she takes funds out of her own IRA.

184. My husband has always done a spousal IRA for me. Can I still contribute to this?

If you are receiving maintenance, this qualifies as compensation and you can contribute to your own IRA within the normal guidelines.

185. My husband has always contributed to a spousal IRA and deducted it from his taxes. Can he deduct the contribution this year if we are divorced this year?

No. If your divorce is final before the end of the tax year, he cannot deduct any contribution you made to your IRA on his tax return.

APPENDIX A

FINAL DIVORCE DECREE

To make sure that your final divorce decree gives you the protection that you want, use this checklist to include those items that pertain to you.

1. **The Divorce Process**
   - Who pays the legal fees?
   - Will the husband pay the legal fees and court costs if the wife must take him to court for non-support or for not complying with the divorce decree? Will there be interest charges?
   - Does the wife want to take back her maiden name?

2. **Property**
   - Who gets which property?
   - Who gets which debt?
   - If the pension is to be divided, has the proper paperwork been prepared?
   - If there is a property settlement note, is it collateralized? Is there interest on it?
   - If you get the house, will you get the whole basis in the house?
   - If you get the house and need to sell it immediately, will you be responsible for the entire capital gains tax?

3. **Maintenance**
   - How much maintenance for how long?
   - If maintenance is not awarded now, can it be awarded later?
   - Will there be life insurance to cover maintenance in the event of the payor's death?

4. **Child Support**
   - How much child support for how long?
   - Will the child support change during college or when visitation times change?
   - Who has custody of the children?
   - What is the visitation schedule?
   - Who pays related expenses for school (transportation, books, etc.) and unusual expenses (lessons, camp, teeth, etc.)?
   - Who will deduct the children on income tax forms?

APPENDIX B

CHECKLIST OF INFORMATION
TO GATHER FOR ATTORNEY

- ❏ Name, address and phone number
- ❏ Business address and phone number
- ❏ Name, address and phone number of other party
- ❏ Dates of birth of each party
- ❏ Names and dates of birth of children
- ❏ Prior marriages of each party and details of termination
- ❏ Children of prior marriages and custodial arrangements
- ❏ Date and place of marriage
- ❏ Length of time you have lived in this state
- ❏ Name and address of lawyer representing other party
- ❏ Existence of prenuptial agreement
- ❏ Grounds for divorce
- ❏ Objectives of each party
- ❏ Date of separation
- ❏ Current employment and income of the parties
- ❏ Education/degrees/training of each party
- ❏ Job history and income potential of each party
- ❏ Employee benefits of each party
- ❏ Retirement or pension plans for each party
- ❏ Joint assets of the parties
- ❏ Liabilities or debt of each party
- ❏ Life insurance of each party
- ❏ Separate or personal assets of each party
- ❏ Incidences of domestic abuse or threats
- ❏ Financial records which include:
  - ❏ Bank statements
  - ❏ Tax returns
  - ❏ Applications for loans
  - ❏ Investment statements

- ❏ Family business records which include:
    - ❏ Type of business
    - ❏ Shareholders
    - ❏ Percent of ownership of business
    - ❏ Bank statements of business
    - ❏ Tax returns of business
    - ❏ Applications for loans
    - ❏ Income and balance sheets
    - ❏ Financial reports

APPENDIX C

ALIMONY/SPOUSAL SUPPORT FACTORS

	Statutory List*	Marital Fault Not Considered	Marital Fault Relevant	Standard of Living	Status as Custodial Parent Considered
Alabama			X	X	
Alaska	X	X		X	X
Arizona	X	X		X	X
Arkansas		X			
California	X	X		X	
Colorado	X	X		X	X
Connecticut	X		X	X	X
Delaware	X	X		X	X
D.C.			X	X	
Florida	X		X	X	
Georgia	X		X	X	
Hawaii	X	X		X	X
Idaho	X		X		
Illinois	X	X		X	X
Indiana	X	X			
Iowa	X	X		X	X
Kansas		X			
Kentucky	X		X[1]	X	
Louisiana	X		X		X
Maine	X	X			
Maryland	X		X	X	
Massachusetts	X		X	X	
Michigan			X	X	
Minnesota	X	X		X	X
Mississippi			X		
Missouri	X		X	X	X
Montana	X	X		X	X
Nebraska	X	X		X	X
Nevada			X	X	X
New Hampshire	X		X	X	X
New Jersey	X		X	X	X

	Statutory List*	Marital Fault Not Considered	Marital Fault Relevant	Standard of Living	Status as Custodial Parent Considered
New Mexico	X	X		X	
New York	X		X	X	X
North Carolina	X		X	X	
North Dakota			X	X	
Ohio	X	X		X	X
Oklahoma		X		X	X
Oregon	X	X		X	X
Pennsylvania	X		X	X	
Rhode Island	X		X	X	X
South Carolina	X		X	X	X
South Dakota			X	X	
Tennessee	X		X	X	X
Texas	X		X	X	X
Utah	X		X	X	X
Vermont	X	X		X	X
Virginia	X		X	X	
Washington	X	X		X	
West Virginia	X		X		X
Wisconsin	X	X		X	X
Wyoming			X		

* Although there is a statutory list of factors, the judge may in its discretion consider other factors under the particular circumstances of the case.
[1] Only fault on the part of the party seeking alimony.

Source: ©The American Bar Association. All rights reserved.
Reprinted by Permission of ABA Publishing: All tables are current as of February 2004.
http://www.abanet.org/family/familylaw/tables.html.

APPENDIX D

CUSTODY CRITERIA

	Statutory Guide-lines	Children's Wishes	Joint Custody	Coop-erative Parent	Domestic Violence	Health	Attorney or GAL
Alabama	X	X	X		X		
Alaska	X	X	X		X		X
Arizona	X	X	X	X	X	X	X
Arkansas					X		
California	X	X		X	X	X	X
Colorado	X	X	X^1	X	X	X	X
Connecticut		X	X				X
Delaware	X	X	X		X	X	X
D.C.	X	X	X	X	X	X	X
Florida	X	X	X	X	X	X	X
Georgia	X	X	X		X		X
Hawaii	X^2	X^8	X^7		X		X^9
Idaho	X	X	X		X	X	
Illinois	X	X	X	X	X	X	X
Indiana	X	X	X	X	X	X	X
Iowa	X	X	X	X	X	X	X
Kansas	X	X	X	X	X	X	
Kentucky	X	X	X	X	X	X	X
Louisiana	X	X	X		X		
Maine	X	X	X		X		X
Maryland		X	X	X	X	X	X
Massachusetts			X		X		X
Michigan	X	X	X	X	X	X	X
Minnesota	X	X	X		X	X	X
Mississippi	X		X			X	X^2
Missouri	X	X	X	X	X	X	X
Montana	X	X	X		X		X
Nebraska	X	X	X		X	X	X
Nevada	X	X	X	X	X		X
New Hampshire	X	X	X		X		X
New Jersey	X	X	X	X	X	X	X
New Mexico	X	X	X	X	X	X	X

	Statutory Guide-lines	Children's Wishes	Joint Custody	Coop-erative Parent	Domestic Violence	Health	Attorney or GAL
New York		X			X^2		X
North Carolina		X^2	X		X	X	
North Dakota	X	X	X	X^3	X	X	
Ohio	X^2	X	X^5		X	X	X
Oklahoma	X	X	X	X	X		X^4
Oregon	X	X	X	X	X		X^3
Pennsylvania	X	X	X	X	X	X	X
Rhode Island		X	X	X	X	X	X
South Carolina		X	X	X	X	X	X
South Dakota		X	X	X	X		
Tennessee	X	X^5	X^6	X	X		X
Texas	X	X	X	X	X	X	X
Utah	X	X	X	X			X
Vermont	X		X		X		X
Virginia	X	X^2	X	X	X	X	X^4
Washington	X	X			X	X	X
West Virginia	X	X	X		X		
Wisconsin	X	X	X	X	X	X	X
Wyoming	X	X	X	X	X	X	

[1] Now uses term "parental rights and responsibilities."

[2] Considered if child is old enough.

[3] By case law.

[4] Not mandatory.

[5] The court must listen to the reasonable preferences of a child twelve or older, giving greater weight to the preferences of older children. The courts may at its discretion hear the reasonable preference of children under the age of twelve.

[6] In divorce, the courts no longer use "custody" terminology, instead, separately allocating between the parents (1) residential time; and, (2) parental responsibility in specific areas such as non-emergency health care, religion, education and extra-curricular activities.

[7] Emphasizes "best interest of child."

[8] If Child is of sufficient age and capacity to reason and form intelligent preference.

[9] Appointment of custody evaluators and guardian ad litem authorized by administrative rule.

CHILD SUPPORT GUIDELINES

	Income Share	Percent of Income	Extraordinary Medical Deduction	Child-care Deduction	College Support	Shared Parenting Time Offset
Alabama	X	X	X^p	X^m	X	
Alaska		X	X^m	X	X	X
Arizona	X		X^m	X^p		
Arkansas		X	X^d	X^d		
California	X		X^m	X^m		X
Colorado	X		X^m	X^m		X
Connecticut	X		X^d		X	
Delaware			X^m	X^m		X^*
D.C.		X	X^d	X	X	X
Florida	X		X^p	X^m		
Georgia		X	X^p	X^m		
Hawaii	X	X	X^{m3}	X	X	X
Idaho	X		X^m	X^p		X
Illinois		X			X	
Indiana	X		X^p	X^m	X	
Iowa	X			X^m	X	X
Kansas	X			X^m		X
Kentucky	X		X^m	X^p		
Louisiana	X		X^m	X^m		
Maine	X		X^m	X^m		
Maryland	X		X^m	X^m		X
Massachusetts		X	X^m	X	X	
Michigan	X		X^m	X^m	X	X
Minnesota		X		X^m		X
Mississippi		X	X^d	X^d		
Missouri	X		X	X	X	X
Montana			X^m	X^m		
Nebraska	X		X^d	X^m		X
Nevada		X	X^m	X^d		X
New Hampshire		X	X^d		X	
New Jersey	X		X^m	X^m	X	X

	Income Share	Percent of Income	Extraordinary Medical Deduction	Child-care Deduction	College Support	Shared Parenting Time Offset
New Mexico	X		X^p	X^m		X
New York	X		X^m	X^m	X	
North Carolina	X	X	X^p	X^m		X
North Dakota		X		X^d		
Ohio	X		X^p	X^m		X^p
Oklahoma	X		X^a	X^m		X
Oregon	X		X^p	X^m	X	X
Pennsylvania	X		$X^{m/d}$	X^m		
Rhode Island	X		X^d	X^m		
South Carolina	X		X^d	X^m	X	
South Dakota	X		X^d	X^d		
Tennessee		X	X^m		X^1	X^2
Texas		X	X^m	X^d		
Utah	X		X^m	$X^{m/p}$		X
Vermont	X		X^m	X^m		X
Virginia	X		X^a	X^a		X
Washington	X		X^m	X^m	X	
West Virginia	X		X^m	X^m		X
Wisconsin		X	X^m	X^d		
Wyoming	X		X^d	X^d		X

* by case law
a mandatory add-ons
m mandatory deduction
p permissive deduction
d deviation factor
1 May be voluntarily agreed by the parties, in which case it is contractually enforceable thereafter, but otherwise may not be imposed by the court. However, an oligor parent may be required to contribute during a child's minority to an educational trust fund which would be used for college costs post-minority.
2 Support may be increased or decreased it the obligor spends more or less than 80 days (the putative normal amount of time) with a child.
3 Credit given for actual cost of health care insurance premium paid for children.

APPENDIX F

GROUNDS FOR DIVORCE AND RESIDENCY REQUIREMENTS

	No Fault Sole Ground	No Fault Added to Traditional	Incom-patibility	Living Separate and Apart	Judicial Separation	Durational Requirements
Alabama		X	X	2 years	X	6 months
Alaska	X		X	2 years	X	6 months
Arizona	X	X[1]			X	90 days
Arkansas		X		18 mos.	X	60 days
California	X				X	6 months*
Colorado	X				X	90 days
Connecticut		X		18 mos.	X	1 year
Delaware		X	X	6 mos.		6 months
D.C.	X			1 year	X	6 months
Florida	X					6 months
Georgia		X				6 months
Hawaii				2 years[3]	X	6 months[4]
Idaho		X			X	6 weeks
Illinois		X		2 years	X	90 days
Indiana		X	X		X	60 days
Iowa	X				X	1 year
Kansas			X		X	60 days
Kentucky	X			60 days	X	180 days
Louisiana		X[1]		6 mos.[2]	X	6 months
Maine		X			X	6 months
Maryland		X		1 year	X	1 year
Massachusetts		X			X	None
Michigan	X				X	6 months
Minnesota	X				X	180 days
Mississippi		X				6 months
Missouri		X		1-2 years	X	90 days
Montana	X		X	180 days	X	90 days
Nebraska	X				X	1 year
Nevada			X	1 year	X	6 weeks
New Hampshire		X		2 years		1 year

	No Fault Sole Ground	No Fault Added to Traditional	Incom-patibility	Living Separate and Apart	Judicial Separation	Durational Requirements
New Jersey		X		18 mos.		1 year
New Mexico		X	X		X	6 months
New York		X		1 year	X	1 year
North Carolina		X		1 year	X	6 months
North Dakota		X			X	6 months
Ohio		X	X	1 year		6 months
Oklahoma			X		X	6 months
Oregon	X				X	6 months
Pennsylvania		X		2 years		6 months
Rhode Island		X		3 years	X	1 year
South Carolina		X		1 year	X	3 months (both residents)
South Dakota		X			X	None
Tennessee		X		2 years	X	6 months
Texas		X		3 years		6 months
Utah		X		3 years		90 days
Vermont		X		6 mos.		6 months
Virginia		X		1 year	X	6 months
Washington	X					1 year
West Virginia		X		1 year	X	1 year
Wisconsin	X				X	6 months
Wyoming		X	X		X	60 days

* California requires domicile as distinguished from residency for jurisdictional purposes.
[1] Covenant marriage statutes establish specific grounds for divorce for covenant marriages.
[2] Two years for covenant marriages.
[3] Grounds are either marriage irretrievably broken or two years separation.
[4] Six months in state and three months in circuit waiting for divorce itself, but can file as soon as residency established.

Source: ©The American Bar Association. All rights reserved.
Reprinted by Permission of ABA Publishing: All tables are current as of February 2004.
http://www.abanet.org/family/familylaw/tables.html

APPENDIX G

PROPERTY DIVISION

	Community Property	Only Marital Divided	Statutory List of Factors	Non-monetary Contributions	Economic Misconduct	Contribution to Education
Alabama		X		X		X
Alaska	X[1]		X	X	X	
Arizona	X				X	X
Arkansas		X	X	X		
California	X		X	X	X	X
Colorado		X	X	X	X	
Connecticut			X	X	X	X
Delaware		X	X	X	X	X
D.C.		X	X	X	X	
Florida		X	X	X	X	X
Georgia		X				
Hawaii	X[4]		X[5]	X[2]	X[3]	
Idaho	X		X			
Illinois		X	X	X	X	
Indiana		X	X	X	X	X
Iowa			X	X	X	X
Kansas			X		X	
Kentucky		X	X	X	X	X
Louisiana	X					
Maine		X	X	X	X	
Maryland		X	X	X	X	
Massachusetts			X	X	X	X
Michigan		X		X	X	X
Minnesota		X	X	X	X	
Mississippi		X	X	X	X	X
Missouri		X	X	X	X	X
Montana			X	X	X	
Nebraska		X		X		
Nevada	X	X		X	X	X
New Hampshire			X	X	X	X
New Jersey		X	X	X	X	X
New Mexico	X					

	Community Property	Only Marital Divided	Statutory List of Factors	Non-monetary Contributions	Economic Misconduct	Contribution to Education
New York		X	X	X	X	X
North Carolina		X	X	X	X	X
North Dakota				X	X	X
Ohio		X	X	X	X	X
Oklahoma		X		X	X	
Oregon				X	X	X
Pennsylvania		X	X	X	X	X
Rhode Island		X	X	X	X	X
South Carolina		X	X	X	X	X
South Dakota				X	X	
Tennessee		X	X	X	X	X
Texas	X				X	
Utah						
Vermont			X	X	X	X
Virginia		X	X	X	X	X
Washington	X		X			
West Virginia		X	X	X	X	X
Wisconsin	X	X	X	X	X	X
Wyoming		X	X	X		

[1] The parties by contract can agree to make some or all of their marital property community property.

[2] During marriage non-monetary contributions do not affect property division nor does the lack of them.

[3] No statutory provision apply; case law is mixed.

[4] During marriage non-monetary contributions do not affect property division, nor does the lack of them.

[5] No statutory provisions; case law is mixed.

Source: ©The American Bar Association. All rights reserved.
Reprinted by Permission of ABA Publishing: All tables are current as of February 2004.
http://www.abanet.org/family/familylaw/tables.html

RESOURCE LIST

ABCs of Divorce for Women, Carol Ann Wilson and Ginita Wall. Boulder. Quantum Press. 2003.

Between Love and Hate: A Guide to Civilized Divorce. Lois Gold. New York. Plume. 1992.

The Boys and Girls Book About Divorce. Richard Gardner. New York. Science House. 1970.

The Consequences of Divorce: Economic and Custodial Impact on Children and Adults. Craig A. Everett. Binghamton, NY. Haworth Press. 1991.

Divorce and Decision Making, A Woman's Guide. Christina Robertson. Chicago. Follett. 1980.

Divorce Decisions Workbook: A Planning and Action Guide. Margorie L. Engel and Diana D. Gould. New York. McGraw Hill. 1992.

Divorce Help Sourcebook. Margorie L. Engel. Detroit. Visible Ink Press. 1994.

Do I Have to Give Up Me to Be Loved By You? Jordon Paul and Margaret. Compcare. 1985.

Dollars and Sense of Divorce. Judith Briles, Edwin Schilling and Carol Ann Wilson. Chicago. Dearborn Financial Publishing. 1998.

Fair Share Divorce for Women. Kathleen Miller. Bellevue, WA. Miller, Bird Advisors. 1995.

Financial Guide To Divorce Settlement, Carol Ann Wilson. Columbia, MD. Marketplace Books. 2000

Financial Planning from We to Me: Divorce Strategies to Help You Get More of What You Want. Kathleen L. Cotton. Lynwood. WA. Wealth Books. 1996.

Friendly Divorce Guidebook for Connecticut, Barbara Kahn Stark. Denver. Bradford Publishing. 1998

Friendly Divorce Guidebook for Colorado, S. W. Whicher and M. Arden Hauer. Denver. Bradford Publishing.

A Guide to Divorce Mediation: How to Reach a Fair, Legal Settlement at a Fraction of the Cost. Gary J. Friedman. New York. Workman Publishing. 1993.

How to Live With Another Person. David Viscott. New York. Pocket Books. 1974.

How to Survive the Loss of a Love. Colgrove, Bloomfield & McWilliams. New York. Leo Press. 1976.

If Only He Knew. Gary Smalley. Zondervan. 1979.

If Only She Knew. Gary Smalley. Zondervan. 1979.

Love For A Lifetime. James Dobson. Waco, Texas. Word Publishing. 1985.

Love Must Be Tough. James Dobson. Waco, Texas. Word Publishing. 1985.

Mom's House, Dad's House: Making Shared Custody Work. Isolina Ricci. New York. McMillan. 1980.

Money Sense: What Every Woman Must Know to Be Financially Confident. Judith Briles. Chicago. Moody. 1995.

The Parents Book About Divorce. Richard Gardner. New York. Doubleday. 1977.

Smart Ways to Save Money During and After Divorce. Victoria Felton-Collins and Ginita Wall. Berkeley, CA. Nolo Press. 1994.

Survival Manual for Men in Divorce, Edwin Schilling III and Carol Ann Wilson. Boulder. Omni Press. 2004

Ten Smart Money Moves for Women. Judith Briles. Chicago. Contemporary Books. 1999.

Why Am I Afraid to Tell You Who I Am? John Powell. Illinois. Argus Communications. 1969.

Women Who Love Too Much. Robin Norwood. Pocket Book Publications. 1985.

You're Entitled: A Divorce Lawyer Talks to Women. Sidney M. DeAngelis. Chicago. Contemporary Books. 1989.

What do computers have to do with divorce?

Quite a lot . . . since Carol Ann Wilson, CFP®, Financial Divorce Specialist, co-author of this book developed divorce planning software. According to divorce experts, what's missing in most divorce processes is financial expertise. The software goes a long way toward filling the need.

As a Certified Financial Planner® and a Financial Divorce Specialist, Carol Ann developed divorce planning software which accounts for all financial assets of the couple and creates a number of scenarios to show how every decision affects both parties for years to come. An easy-to-understand set of graphs shows how each spouse's income and assets change over time.

This system allows both partners, as well as the judge, to have a clearer view of their financial futures. All that is necessary to develop a series of projections is a completed questionnaire.

Example: A single-income divorce.

John and Jane are 40 years old and have two children. They own a home worth $165,000 with net equity of $77,000. Their IRAs and 401(k) plan total $165,000 in value. John's take-home pay is $68,760 a year.

The following settlement has been suggested. After the divorce, Jane and the children will live in the house, which will be deeded to her. She will also receive $44,000 of the retirement moneys and John $121,500, thus dividing the assets equally. John will pay Jane alimony of $600 per month for 5 years and child support. He will also pay college costs which start in 4 years.

At first glance this looks like a fair settlement. But the graph tells a different story. Within seven years, Jane's assets will be depleted, while John's investments will have grown dramatically. (See Figure 1.)

The DivorceCalc™ Proposal

DivorceCalc projections suggest higher maintenance for ten years and a disproportional split of assets, combined with lowered expense for Jane. This scenario would result in an equitable situation for both parties. (See Figure 2.)

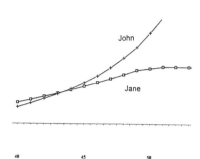

A Financial Divorce Specialist can provide you with this expertise. Financial Divorce Specialists are financial professionals who have successfully completed an intensive training program on the complex financial issues of divorce and on the divorce planning software. For a qualified Financial Divorce Specialist in your area, call toll-free 888-332-3342 or visit www.FinancialDivorceAssociation.com. Note: All Financial Divorce Specialists set their own fee schedule.

Please feel free to have your own lawyer call the Financial Divorce Association to discuss your computer generated scenarios. Financial Divorce Specialists have considerable experience, both in and out of court, that may be helpful to your lawyer. They can even appear as an expert witness on your behalf.

Financial Divorce Association, Inc.
Box 11276
Boulder, CO 80301
303-774-1225
888-332-3342